The Resurrection of the Body

Michael Schmidt was born in Mexico in 1947. He studied at Harvard and at Wadham College, Oxford. He is currently Professor of Poetry at Glasgow University, where he is convenor of the Creative Writing M.Litt programme. He is a founder (1969) and editorial and managing director of Carcanet Press Limited, and a founder (1972) and general editor of PN Review. A Fellow of the Royal Society of Literature, he received an O.B.E. in 2006 for services to poetry.

Books by Michael Schmidt include

Poetry
Selected Poems, Smith/Doorstop, 1997
The Love of Strangers, Century Hutchinson, 1989
Choosing a Guest: new and selected poems, Anvil, 1983

Poetry Anthologies
New Poetries I-IV, Carcanet, 1994-2007
The Harvill Book of Twentieth-Century Poetry in English, Harvill, 1999
Poets on Poets (with Nick Rennison), Waterstone's/Carcanet, 1997
A Calendar of Modern Poetry, PN Review 100, 1994
Eleven British Poets, Methuen/Routledge, 1980

Novels
The Colonist, Muller/Hutchinson, 1983
The Dresden Gate, Century Hutchinson, 1988

Translations
On Poets & Others, Octavio Paz, Paladin, 1991
Flower & Song: Nahuatl Poetry (with Edward Kissam), Anvil, 1977

Literary History and Criticism
Lives of the Ancient Poets: The Greeks, Weidenfeld, 2004
The Story of Poetry I-IV, Weidenfeld, 2001-2008
Lives of the Poets, Weidenfeld, 1998
Reading Modern Poetry, Routledge, 1989
Fifty Modern British Poets: an introduction, Pan/Heinemann, 1979
Fifty English Poets 1300-1900: an introduction, Pan/Heinemann, 1979

The Resurrection of the Body

Michael Schmidt

...And as in winter leavès been bereft,
Each after other, till the tree be bare,
So that there n'is but bark and branch yleft,
Lieth Troilus, bereft of each welfare,
Ybounden in the blackè bark of care,
Disposèd wood out of his wit to breyde,
So sore him sat the changing of Criseyde.
Chaucer Troilus and Crisseyde
Book IV, lines 225-231

Smith/Doorstop Books

For Angel Garcia-Gomez, these fictions

'His Father was a Baker' appeared in *Selected Poems*. 'The Golden Dome' was published in *The Times*. Other poems appeared in *Critical Quarterly*, *London Magazine*, *The North*, *Oxford Poetry*, *Poetry Review*, and *The Reader*.

Published 2007 by
Smith/Doorstop Books
The Poetry Business
The Studio
Byram Arcade
Westgate
Huddersfield HD1 1ND

British Library Cataloguing-in-Publication Data. A catalogue record for this book is available from the British Library.

Designed and typeset at The Poetry Business
Printed by Charlesworths, Wakefield
Author's photograph by Benedict Schmidt

The front cover image, part of 'The Resurrection, Cookham' by Stanley Spencer, is reproduced by kind permission of Tate Britain.

Distributed by Central Books Ltd., 99 Wallis Road, London E9 5LN

The Poetry Business gratefully acknowledges the help of Arts Council England and Kirklees Cultural Services.

CONTENTS

7	Pangur Bàn
9	Iberian Clichés
13	Don Juan
15	Nine Witches
18	Jacob and the Angel
20	The Resurrection of the Body
23	Furniture for a Ballad
26	Between
28	Not Yet
30	Between Birnam Wood and Dunsinane
32	Third Persons
33	Conceit
34	'His father was a baker …'
36	Cuernavaca Ghazal
38	A Red Grove
41	The Outer Trench
44	Amphion
47	Wanting to Think
48	John Gilpin Eludes the Hunt
50	Victor Casasola, Photographer
53	Erebus and Terror
56	The Golden Dome
59	Regression
62	Notes for the Cactus Poem
63	Inordinate Desires

Pangur Bàn

i.

Jerome has his enormous dozy lion.
Myself, I have a cat, my Pangur Bàn.

What did Jerome feed up his lion with?
Always he's fat and fleecy, always sleeping

As if after a meal. Perhaps a Christian?
Perhaps a lamb, or a fish, or a loaf of bread.

His lion's always smiling, chin on paw,
What looks like purring rippling his face

And there on Jerome's escritoire by the quill and ink pot
The long black thorn he drew from the lion's paw.

Look, Pangur, at the picture of the lion –
Not a mouser like you, not lean, not ever

Chasing a quill as it flutters over parchment
Leaving its trail that is the word of God.

Pangur, you are so trim beside the lion.
– Unlike Jerome in the mouth of his desert cave

Wrapped in a wardrobe of robes despite the heat,
I in this Irish winter, Pangur Bàn,

Am cold, without so much as your pillow case
Of fur, white, with ginger tips on ears and tail.

ii.

My name is neither here nor there, I am employed
By Colum Cille who will be a saint

Because of me and how I have set down
The word of God. He pays. He goes to heaven.

I stay on earth, in this cell with the high empty window,
The long light in summer, the winter stars.

I work with my quill and colours, bent and blinder
Each season, colder, but the pages fill.

Just when I started work the cat arrived
Sleek and sharp at my elbow, out of nowhere;

I dipped my pen. He settled in with me.
He listened and replied. He kept my counsel.

                iii.

Here in the margin, Pangur, I inscribe you.
Almost Amen. Prowl out of now and go down

Into time's garden, wary with your tip-toe hearing.
You'll live well enough on mice and shrews till you find

The next scriptorium, a bowl of milk. Some scribe
Will recognise you, Pangur Bàn, and feed you;

You'll find your way to him as you did to me
From nowhere (but you sniffed out your Jerome).

Stay by him, too, until his Gospel's done.
(I linger over John, the closing verses,

You're restless, won't be touched. I'm old. The solstice.)
Amen, dear Pangur Bàn. Amen. Be sly.

Iberian Clichés

i. *At home*

A Spaniard painted the blue cow,
The dachshund and the Magdalen's crotch;
The midget with the giant prick
Is who he wished himself to be
At times, a function not a man.
He painted to discover what
The time of day, the appetite,
What was his hunger and his thirst,
Each canvas effortless with pain,
A portrait of the ones he was
Just at that hour, night or day.
To hold the bird that was the brush
Light in his fingers with its song!
To feel the heartbeat in his wrist,
His wrist alive upon its bough!
The flapping wind that beats the tree
Blows from the heart; the viscera
Root him, he moves with all his roots
Painting the cow he sees as blue,
The dachshund yapping at his heels
Familiar but not yet his own,
A penis on its four short legs
Trotting beside, sniffing a trunk;
The Magdalen who has yet to meet
Christ in the long cold room of want
And whom he loves with all his flesh
Except the heart which will belong
Always to him and him alone,
Fluttering the hair upon his chest.

ii. *Corrida*

He lifts the wine-skin in the sun
And runs the stream between his lips.
Meanwhile the Macarena plays,
The bull's cavorting with a horse.
The sand like canvas takes the daubs
Of blood and excrement, the crowd
Cheers and the wine jet fills his throat
Until his heart is floating on
A bleary sea, the enormous sun
Touching the stream as if it's blood.
He wipes his famous fist across
His famous lips and thinks it's time.
He takes the woman at his side
With her hot eyes and heavy hair
Back to his studio.
                            Left behind,
The bull's arrested in the red
Deep cape, for ever: memory,
Lost in its rage and pain, its head
Under the matador's right arm.
The dancing testicles are still
In their long sack, the rump is firm;
The banderillas in his neck,
Blue, red and pink, a slime of blood
Like something intimate, obscene,
On the huge blackness of his chest
As if he was a shadow not
The substance of the Miura hills.
A black bull and its shadow grown
Together cannot be unpicked.
The artist's eye has left the scene,
Floating on air, on wine and lust.
Here there is nothing but a crowd,
A dying bull, a ring of dust.

iii. *Los Gallos*

The cocks are spurred. Their coral combs
Stiff, and all rage their tacks of eyes,
A hush. The bell. They are released
And crash together as if in love
To claw the eye, the throat, the heart.

His money's on the smaller bird
Because he liked the noise he made
Deep in his throat before the fight,
As if he had a purpose, love,
As if he called to her aloud,

As if his hen or hens could hear
His reassuring, husky voice
When, settling on their roost, they thought
Where is he? Has the moon come out?
They crash together as if in love.

He does not wait to see who wins
For fear his little bird might fare
Badly and have his gold neck wrung
In shame by the fat proprietor
With the cigar and bandaged hand.

He goes back to his studio
And leaves the two cocks in the air
Frozen forever on the point
Of death or victory. He makes
Out of their bluster an ideogram

Of violence which has found form
And finding form finds balance, too,
And in the balance figures live
Moving in stillness, still in their dance,
Deep in their chests a sound like love.

11

Deep in his throat the smaller cock
(This is the lie that tells the truth)
Could feel the workings of his heart.
His trainer with a little twist
Unsheathed the spur and tried the blade.

He put the cock's face to his lips
And blew on him as if a coal,
Then threw him at the unpainted sand
To seer it with his furious knife
And daub it here and there with blood.

Was there shouting in the stands?
Each man invents in a staged death
A prize, a victory, a kiss.
In the high studio the cocks suspend
Greed and arousal, elegy.

These are two cocks a Chinese sage
Might, with a brush and pot of ink,
Casually admit to sense
As if they were in fact the word
For such convergent energies,

A human crowd aroused by blood,
The striving birds, the piles of coin,
The smell of sand and leather, smoke,
The tinny music amplified,
The crow of the surviving cock.

An alphabet cannot reveal
The gist, for sound is not enough
To render sense, the sense of love
Or violence, of what is there
And in its being does not mean.

Don Juan

In his cotton shorts, white stockings, his brass-buckled boots,
The dunes came home, in his scalp, in the tight corners
Of his blue eyes. How they brushed and froted him,
His nurse, his elder sister, the hairlipped house-maid,
First dry then wet, with a big striped towel, red and white
Like a barber's, but he did not bleed, just a few
Scratches on cheek and back, though he cried; he cried
As if they'd sanded him down, as if they'd flayed him.

Never again did he go to the beach and never
Swam (because he could swim) again with bright
Mermaids, though he was to remember, to dream
The suck of their lips, the shimmer of their blue tails,
And their hair that was green and silver, their cool breasts
Which they said he could touch, which they held up for his kiss,
Which were firm and round like no fruit he'd ever seen
Or touched or tasted, the nipples sweet and darker,
Sweet in a way he'd not known things could be sweet,
Darker and pointed, a skin like the skin of his lips.
He felt for their legs, long legs, but they had no legs,
Only the handsome flipper, the graceful tail
Where the scales were soft as velvet and stroked both ways,
Silver to turquoise, turquoise back to silver;
They gazed at him as he stroked them in the sea.

Had it not been for the sand
He would have returned among them, would have become
A merman, not a poor forked creature, would have been known
As a mender of easy hearts, a man who made love
As other men make shoes, or music, or cheeses.
But sand got into the blood, silted the heart;
Now the cinders hurt under his ribs, they're still red hot
From his eternal banquet with the stone

Host, his father-in-law, and the horse and the plinth
And the list of discarded wives he can't call to mind
As a face, a voice, a scent, or a taste on the tongue
Though he has an ever after to hunt them down.

The roads of his country are paved
With what at first look like cobbles, but are in fact
The half-shells of broken hearts. A traffic of carts
Going home bumps over them, the drivers
Boys who not once knew their father, or why in their own hearts
Sand is, and cinders, hot, and a gnawing as of rats
About their groins, like desire, like hunger and hurt.
They would be handsome if in the blind window frames
A girl appeared, vague with dreaming, a mermaid,
And came into focus, focussed, they could be men,
The man their father was intended to be.

At home the women wear black, their faces are veiled.
They don't smile, though they once did. They live on their knees.
And the boys drive their carts on the roads home past the bay.
They do not swim. No face out of the waves
Watches them with desire, the sea turns away. It sucks
The shingle and spits; sucks, then spits again.

Nine Witches

A long way after a passage in Ben Jonson's Masque of Queens,
2 February 1609

i.

The raven I had tucked beneath my arm,
He scritched and scritched. I took his head in hand
And broke the voice off with a little twist.
I have the beak, the tongue; one curving wing
To fan the fire, raise a breeze, or shade the eyes
If the moon glares white hot and the sparking stars.

ii.

I've been among the mammals gathering off
The rabid wolf's chin slather; a doe's scut, bristles
From a fox's cheek, the raisins rabbits drop
Up on the moor. Asleep in the gorse and thorn I found
Your fool cat Scruple, her belly full of mouse and shrew.
Here she is, sharp and scowling in the burlap sack.

iii.

I lay along the furrow where wheat is newly sown.
I heard thaw in the soil, the earthworms moving, moles
Waking in their dark tunnels, mending their ways.
It was dark with heavy water, zero stars.
From my throat I gargled out the mildew spell.
My shoes and cloak and fists are full of wheat seed.

iv.

I have been to the Euphrates gathering skulls
Quite fresh, the faces on them, the wide eyes
Still full of tears. I gathered them in public highways,
Back gardens, mosques, cars, ditches, hospitals.
Three dozen here are threaded on barbed wire,
All I could drag back. I'll get more in tomorrow.

v.

It was so cool all day beneath the cradle.
I almost slept the baby's sleep; when the night was still
I sucked her breath, I breathed her breathing in,
So fresh it was, and sweet, I held it close
Until her fitful body like the night outside
Fell calm. I held it till I got back here.

vi.

I had a knife when I went down the mountain.
I marked my destination with a cross.
I found Avila: the woman bent in prayer,
Teresa, Saint: *to pray is labour, making prayer*
A holy act like stirring soup, or weaving, sweeping.
I slit her weaving, diced her prayer, I swept her up.

vii.

The murderer was dangling from his noose, out
On the high road by the gibbet (the watchman snored).
Veins watered him a week ago, run dry now.
He sagged, was sallow, peck marks in his eyes.
I stole the shirt and let the ribs show through,
The trousers and the shoes, left him forked and human.

viii.

The screech owl laid nine eggs in my pointed hat,
Bedding them with black down from her breast and tail.
She stayed with them until the moon went up:
She climbed the steep sky with it, screaming, circling.
I took my stinking hat and flew for home
Faster than bird of prey. A soufflé, sisters?

ix.

The latest, the new, the novice witch am I.
I went abroad tonight for apprentice things,
Poppies, hemlock, hen-bane, libbards-bane,

16

Wild fig from graves, snails, toads and sarin, roaches.
I did not intend to find peach, pear or apple
Or the god of love perched in a loquat laughing.

I stole his bow, his blindfold, his winged shoes;
I took his laughter and I left him there
Stricken on his bough, eyes vacant, stopped
As a clockwork bird run down, as a toy outgrown,
Or a child who dreamt he was free but woke up stone.
I share out the laugh with my sisters. We jig on the heath.

Jacob and the Angel

*And when he saw that he prevailed not against him, he
touched the hollow of his thigh; and the hollow of Jacob's thigh
was strained, as he wrestled with him.*
                    Genesis *32.xxv*

'He fell into the darkness and I caught him.
His eyes were closed, he did not wish to see
A man embrace him, he being an angel.
As long as he kept his eyes shut his lips could sing
Against my skin, he was so new, his hair
Feathering at the nape, his chest and sides
Smooth, his legs and thighs, not a hint of down,
An aura merely, the face rapt with desire.
What colour were his eyes? He kept them closed,
Like Cupid, blind, and would not meet my eye.

'That was the wrestle I had with the angel.
It was not about naming. I witnessed him,
Each inch of him I touched and kissed and loved
But he, who took the worship from my fingers,
Who drained me of desire, who made me love,
Left, though I held him hard, left though I held him,
Eyes screwed tight shut, bolted down, he went
Out of my arms like vapour, like a sigh.

'They say we wrestled: he came down and challenged.
It is not so. I had been there already
Almost asleep, he fell into my arms
And how could I not love him? Let me say:
He was an angel but he had no wings;
He was light and luminous and left behind
A darkness and a blindness, I was blind
Because he did not look at me or name me.
Imagine that: my fingers on his face

Could not prise up his eyes. We lay there breathing
After a long night. That's when they found us
And tried the story out that we'd been wrestling,
He was an angel, I was Jacob. He changed my name.
I said it had been so and he said nothing.
He was away, trailing his shirt, he vanished.
I said it had been so, yes, he had named me.

'The place I called Peniel because I saw
God's face and lived, and lived to tell the story.
I did not see his eyes, though, just his face,'
And the sun rose upon him and he passed over.

The Resurrection of the Body

...So will I melt into a bath to washe them in my bloode...
S. Robert Southwell S.J.

The cellar floor is swept. Women are weeping
Like shadows in torchlight, around the straw pallet they hover,
The soon-to-be-mourners, a dozen, discarding their shawls,
Unpinning their hair. It's so hot in the cellar of death.
Professional, they know what's to come:
She will shrug, shiver, jaw drop open, let go.

Led out of blinding daylight the Healer comes down.
He raises his hand and stills the scrum of women.
He comes down like a lamp into a cavern,
Gathering from sweltering noon light a cool glow.
He comes as if out of the desert sequinned with dew
And his gaze, austere, not unkind, goes through the women
Settling on the parched form stretched on the pallet,
Human, almost beyond pain, but not a child.
The man did say *child* but she is almost a woman,
Her delicate feet, long legs, the down at her crotch,
Flat belly, firm, the handsome small domes of her breasts
Panting, panting, not a child, though her father, grieving,
Insists, believing, a child. So he says to her, *child*.

She focuses her dark gaze on his amazing pallor,
Her fever like a bruise against him. She closes her lips
Reaching for a sheet, the rolled winding sheet, for cover
But he makes her calm, she understands, her lips now parted
Rapt, she holds her breath (she has breath to hold now).
She watches him, he bends down to her, to lift her up,
His shirt falls open, she sees where the wounds will be.

What does he feel when he gathers her hot and shivering
Off the pallet, hardly a weight, so smooth, and all

20

The smells upon her, faeces and stale sweat, the scent
Of her scalp, and her breath quite sweet, a surprise;
That hot smooth flesh, that shit and flowers, urine
And something else; and the haze of down on her arms
Up to the elbows, then the quite smooth darkness,
Substance of shadow, her flesh, so smooth, and the breathing
Not weary or fretful now in that limp body;
What does he feel, seeing his own white arm beneath her dark hair,
When he knows what he holds, and what it does to his legs,
To his groin, his bowels, to his rapid heart? He holds her
And out of his chest where she is pressed against him
Flows that unusual grace which is rooted in muscle,
Which comes from the marrow and lymph, which is divine,
The grace of a man whom love has turned into God,
The love of incarnate God whose flesh knows the name of his creature.
He holds her the way his mother will soon cradle him,
Passion giving life, or love; and then compassion.

And what does she feel? Who can know what she feels?
What you would feel, or I, pressed close to his chest,
To his cool skin, his smell of the dust of the road,
Of hearth fires, of wine, the touch of his hair, of bread…
What does she feel? She feels love, she feels his desire
Confusing her, desire but not need, he holds her
Tenderly, his lips to her shoulder and hair.

Out of the cellar he bears her into the air
Shedding her pestilence and the sun dissolves it.
A crowd has assembled. He walks among the crowd
With his light burden, they watch and withdraw, afraid,
Conjuror, they see the girl gaze in his eyes.

At the well he sets her down, she can stand on her own.
At the well she stands straight as a reed and Jesus bathes her,
First her hair, he pours water from a hollowed gourd,
Then her ears and eyes and lips, her face, her neck,

Her heart and hands, her back, her belly, her long thighs,
He washes her feet as if she were a child.
The fever has passed. She calls him *father, father*
Though the man who is her father stands beside him.
She calls him *father*. He wraps her in his own shirt.

Furniture for a Ballad

Mas, ¡ay Madre de piedad!,
que sobre la cruz le tienden,
para tomar la medida
por donde los clavos entren.
Lope de Vega

The standing stone, the stricken tree,
The sheep among, who leave their wool,
Who crop and tup, and drop their lambs,
Into a storm, beneath a moon…

The rider on his foaming horse
At night, to ship, to tryst, to tomb,
Or to a battlefield to find
The long corpse of his broken lord…

And in Dunfermline swilling wine
Another lord who sneers and wipes
His signet hand across his jowl,
Calls for his whore, his harp, his hound…

The new moon rocks the old, old moon
In its bowed arms, as if a child;
The old moon fades into a bruise,
The new moon fattens on its pain.

And who is she there on the prow
Of castle, town, of manse or grange
Gazing in dread that it is death
She sees, her lover on the heath

Coming to her to breathe his last
Into her mouth, a kiss, a cough;
She hungers for him and that breath
He feeds her at a stanza's end,

So like a host upon the tongue
And in his side a gash, his feet
Holed, and his hands. Don't call him Christ.
Leave him unnamed and cradle him.

The borders, marches deep in furze,
The dripping rocks, the swelling moor,
The stricken tree, all see him pass
On his high steed. Is he the Word?

He rides away and leaves deep cloud,
A fleece of grace, the woman still
High on the prow, her arms awake
To catch him living, hold him dead.

He travels south, where he will climb
A higher cross than any here.
Though he passed here and everywhere,
He took his blood and bread away

To Palestine, where prophets said
He'd live and die and rise again.
Within the ballad death is death.
It cannot pray, it can't believe.

And yet it might go after him,
Bear him back to stretch him here
Because of love, because of love,
The night, the maid, the sheep among.

A ballad cannot raise the dead.
It grieves and kills, it grieves again.
Let her in the blown midnight wait
Like a new moon imbibing pain.

Thus he will live and she expect
His visit and her ravishment,

His lips, the thunder of his pulse,
Her handsome womb his citadel...

Leave metaphysics to the Jews.
The crofter minds his wretched sheep,
The lord is rusting in the rain,
The woman stifles a fat yawn,

Goes in, sits down, he has not come.
She drinks a potion, sleeps and dreams,
The standing stone, the stricken tree,
Into a storm, beneath a moon...

We lose her as the night resigns
And so it is, the ballad's made
Out of such furniture as these,
The dripping fern, a daylight moon.

Between

The arrow thirled right through,
The feathers – white as it flew,
Red when it struck the tree –
Stayed like a grafted bough.

A bird perched on the end
Whetting its yellow beak,
Stuck in blood as in lime
Flapped, flailed. Another slain.

*

Buy metamorphosis from Rome:
A tree the cross, and wine the blood,
Bread the flesh, or gingerbread:
The truth is neither this nor that

But what's amid, whatever is
Between a tattered coat and age,
Between a lion and a king,
Leviathan and Lucifer,

A fletched arrow and a bird,
Quicklime and blood, a flapping wing
And life itself, a bow and love:
Call them two dots: the line between.

Language can never quite translate
The motion there or draw the line.
That's where the mystery abides:
The process, not the A or B,

The place where substance (alchemy!)
Transforms and cannot be turned back;

The wine is salty in the wound,
The loaf is baking on the cross.

It is not only Christ who's given
Such bold transitions, such regrets,
To hold him in our hands and mouths,
To swallow and ourselves become.

                *

If we should find ourselves alone
Inside the cave of Proteus
Whether a woman or a man
The creature is, divine or brute,

It is the squeeze and punch and hug,
The gasp and grasp, the pinch and pull,
It is the kiss, the holding close,
And not the lover cowled in weed

Or what it was when you embraced
First in the half-light of the cave,
The water lapping at your thighs,
The smell of fish and excrement.

It's not the radiance finally
You hold; but rather, how you got
From it to him or her, to you,
Is where the mystery abides.

Not Yet

My father said he'd have to cut the tree down,
It was so high and broad at the top, and it leaned
In towards the house so that in wind it brushed
The roof slates, gables and the chimney stone
Leaving its marks there as if with intent.

We said, don't cut it yet, because the tree was so full
Of big and little nests, of stippled fruit.
In spring and summer it spoke in a thousand voices,
The chicks upturned for love, the birds like fishes
Swimming among the boughs, and always talking.

And then a day came when the chicks woke up.
Love was all over, they tumbled from their nests
Into the air, ricocheted from a leaf, a branch,
Almost hit the ground, then found their wings
And soared up crying, brothers, sisters, crying.

Then the nests were vacant. Now we must cut the tree,
My father said. Again we begged, not yet,
Because with autumn the freckled fruit began
To turn to red, to gold, like glowing lamps
Fuelled with sweetness filtered from the soil

And scent that was musk and orange, peach and rose.
And when they dropped (they grew on the topmost branches,
Could not be picked, we took when it was offered)
We wiped them clean and sliced out the darkening bruise
Where they'd bounced on the yellow lawn, by then quite hard

With winter coming. The fruit were so much more than sweet,
Eve fell for such fruit and took Adam with her:
No serpent whispered, no god patrolled the garden.

Only my father. Again, not yet, we said, remembering
What winter had to do with our huge bent tree,

Once it had got the leaves off. We knew the hoar-frost
Tracery and the three-foot icicles
And how it simply was, the December moon
Lighted upon it and hung in its arms like a child.
Not yet, we said, not yet. And my father died,

And the tree swept the slates clean with its wings.
The birds were back and nesting, it was spring,
And nothing had altered much, not yet, not yet.

Between Birnam Wood and Dunsinane

His nightshirt wet with dew, how far had he
Been walking in his sleep? (You could just see
Dawn starting to stir colour in the east.

The moon hung on the sky bald as a cobble,
Giving no light, no music in its sphere.
Round it was, just round, it was just round.)

His feet were shod in mud from field and forest.
He had sat down in the needles and woke up
And wondered where his pillow was, and why

The cold was in him, deep-fixed, like a bone
Right up his spine; had he not seen indeed
In his sleep-walk, out walking the wild Lady

Wringing her hands and washing them with mud,
Her route traced through murder, not all the perfumes
Of Araby, dead moonlight, nor the breeze…

Had he not stopped her, cupped her cold small hands
In his to share the stain, and did she not sigh,
Handing it to him with a tremor of love?

Then had he not kissed her and walked on
And found the bloody Lord in the forest of desire
Who seeing a young man stray among breathing boughs

Waylaid him, embraced and held him close
Drinking the scent of sleep from his scalp and touching
His chest, his belly and his thighs with love?

Best, in love, always to walk that way, asleep,
The eyes wide open, and the heart, as here,
Unwilling to appraise effect or cause,

Reflect how on the one hand, on the other,
To count to two (because he was in love
With two, with him, with her, and when he loved

The one, he loved the other while sleep held),
So long as he did not wake in the muddy furrow
Or on the needles of the forest bed.

Finding his feet and fingers stiff with cold,
Desire in negative, no Lady, no Lord,
No fairy tale, no more *and so they lived*,

Waking in the arrest of heart and head,
Of hope, his hand frozen in his lap,
What could he tell but say the thing he saw:

She vanished white and mumbling in a mist,
His Lady; he recoiled and sought the Lord
Who faded in the dark, his heartbeat marching

The way he went back down among the trees.
They'd left, alone, together. Daylight said
There'll be no happy ever after, ever.

Third Persons

If only he hadn't answered the door when she knocked,
      The phone when she called,
If when he started to write his most brilliant story
      He'd expunged her arrival,
Choosing instead to introduce an easier lover
      Or, in place of marriage, travel…

It's chilling to witness her coming, her hand on the knocker.
      He was older, maybe, settled.
She came with tears and charm and magic perhaps.
      I don't recall. Startled
Into a posture of love, and grateful (she was, after all,
      Young, beautiful),

He embraced her and for a decade, more, let himself believe
      He loved her, even after
Her eyes turned, and her head, in so many obvious directions
      And her laughter
Spread like pink blossom over numerous other lawns,
      Spread deeper and softer,

And blithely she gave herself up to many surprises of love.
      He could not finish it.
He could not close the poisoned chapter. He could not breathe.
      He gave her the benefit
Of every single, every single doubt, resisting, yet at last
      He threw the story out.

Conceit

She spun a line. She knew he was listening to her.
She spun it and he took the fraying ends.
Whatever she was saying, it was cotton,

Then as he rolled the thread between
Forefinger and thumb it turned to silk,
And as he took the needle up to thread it

The line she spun became thin finest gold.
He knew not to believe her but he took it
Because she kept on spinning like the truth

Was ravelling from her lips; he watched her lips.
Cotton, silk and gold, she wanted him
To take the line and sew the wound right up

Although she held the blade still in her hand
Behind her back, and it was dripping, steaming.
There under his left arm the gash lay open

Like a mouth in disbelief. And he believed her.

'His father was a baker ...'

    for A.G.G

His father was a baker, he the youngest son.
I understand they beat him, and they loved him.

His father was a baker in Oaxaca:
I understand his bakery was the best

And his three sons and all his daughters helped
As children with the baking and the pigs.

I can imagine chickens in their patio,
At Christmastime a wattled turkey-cock, a dog

Weathered like a wash-board, yellow-eyed,
That no one stroked, but ate the scraps of bread

And yapped to earn its keep. I understand
The family prospered though the father drank

And now the second brother follows suit.
I understand as well that love came

Early, bladed, and then went away
And came again in other forms, some foreign,

And took him by the heart away from home.
His father was a baker in Oaxaca

And here I smell the loaves that rose in ovens
Throughout a childhood not yet quite complete

And smell the fragrance of his jet-black hair,
Taste his sweet dialect that is mine too,

Until I understand I am to be a baker,
Up before dawn with trays and trays of dough

To feed him this day, next day and for ever –
Or for a time – the honey-coloured loaves.

Cuernavaca Ghazal

i.
Now I remember why we came back here.
The poor, the rich, the gulf of love between them.

ii.
You who were poor are rich now. What to do?
What will you build, how make more money, who will you hurt?

iii.
I have come back to watch, as I did when a child
And my father who loved these people made our fortune.

iv.
Let's not beat about the bush. It's evening. Autumn.
The bush is burning with two birds inside it.

v.
What does autumn mean in a place with so few trees,
Where the leaves bud red and yellow, and no winter follows?

vi.
She's the weaver's widow, he's the butcher with his huge flat blade.
The fruiterer sells pomegranates. Twelve seeds. Dis.

vii.
If so, am I Persephone? Eurydice? Are you?
Then am I Ceres, love, or Orpheus?

viii.
How the workmen sweat! Up and down your ladders with stones,
Like ants with hods, like angry and almost articulate insects.

ix.

The postman comes. Not even a card from exile.
We are home indeed, forgotten among our people.

x.

When the flood ebbed then, it left the world laved, renewed.
Next time the mud will be as deep as mountains.

xi.

The river parched, and there are schools of smooth stones
Shimmering, breathing, on their slow way south.

xii.

We are travelling at different speeds, love, in this orbit,
Your sleep and my sleep, love, remote as planets.

xiii.

I want to leave home now as I did then
But more so, to go, to leave home now for ever.

xiv.

Even your lips taste different – not new, not treacherous;
They taste of before me; they forget our language.

xv.

Leaving you, love, I take less than I ever took before,
Less clothing, much less time this time, and love.

A Red Grove

And in what hour of beauty, in what good arms,
Shall I those regions and that city attain
From whence my dreams and slightest movements rise?
And what good Arms shall take them away again?
                                    Henry Reed

i.

Lisbon first. I saw it from the sky,
Circling where it gathered
Tight by the river, the teeming central plaza,
Moorings wide by the wide boat-speckled water
And the long ugly
Bridge to Setubal, where yellow grapes
Grow to the sugary wine. A bridge
Going somewhere else, and railway lines
Arrowing into shadows cast by clouds.

I knew I'd need to buy a map of Lisbon.
Seven hills, though Virgil never walked there,
A river signifying things all over, all the sloops
And caravels departed; castle, tower,
A ring of tawdry highways. Seen before,
I saw again Lisbon sliced by the plane's wing.
Prosperity had turned it to a maze.
I needed to acquire a map, knowing the way
In the past only, but when the plane touched down
The map was overpriced and I was lost.

ii.

Space holds few surprises for a seasoned traveller.
Time, on the other hand, searched for
From a lighted spot in a row of flying portholes,
Can't be seen. It gives up nothing, doesn't hint

Who will fall from a window, fall ill, or in love.

The Hotel Presidente lift smelled stale
As if it had held its breath. It ascended inch by inch
To five when I depressed the fourth floor button.
There you came on board.
You had black hair, shadow eyes. 'You must be...'
You named me and at once I knew who I was
Like a beast Eve named, who stumbled, stood
On wobbly legs and shook his antlered head
Gazing to left and right at Paradise.
He knew because she named him that he lived.

You'd wound the clock with a sentence. Time began:
It was in that lift the second hand, the minute,
The hour hand began circling, to entrance
Lover-like our few allotted hours, though on that
Occasion the marvel was still in the making, each
Whispering privately, and our time whispering too,
The three of us going down in the dim Otis lift,
Unsure, developing like old black and whites.

iii.

Hold still, I say, looking back, hold still and I'll hold you.
Time says *No. Hold still? I'm not a camera. I never
Held still, not for Antony and not for Abelard.*
The map I bought at the airport before my return,
When you'd already gone, unfolds, is empty.
All those streets and squares but not a tree,
A park, an hotel, an elevation,
Not a kiss on the palm or heart.

Distinct, erratic pulses had measured our time
Until they converged for a night and day.
The map if I could focus through the haze

That fills my eyes, shows where we stayed, just there,
And in that tight square almost
Obliterated by the name of an avenue
Where the Metro stopped, was where I lay
By your heart, pressed lips to your ear,
My ear to your breast. I heard
A music out of you, a rise and fall,
And that's the place we solely occupied.

Forests are between us. Hold that tree
And I hold this; or the end of that cloud,
I'll tug here and I touch you. Rain and rain.
From the luminous peak high over Sintra,
The Atlantic spread before us its violet train.
In the royal fountain we paid above the odds,
Our obols to the 'Saint of Blessed Returns'.

We need returns. I am tired, old and in love
In a red grove of camellia blossom.
You said it was rose petals. It was not.
We argued with our tongues but the pulse
Said I am with you. Yours said so, mine said so.
My dreams and smallest movements take shape there.

The Outer Trench

i.

He dug the ewer up. It was choked with clay.
He worked loose the gouts and pebbles, tipped them out
Like sweet Falerian freed from the baked throat.

Emptied, he held it to his lips and blew
Across the rim and made a Roman sound
Then held it to his ear, a Roman tide;

And when he tipped it up again out flowed
As a libation dark musk-scented wine
As from a wound leaps blood eager for air,

A wound in the throat of an old foe, harvested
Out in the red dune-fields of Africa,
Carthago, and the blood is salt, and crusts;

Or it's wine that bubbles out of a chuckling crater,
Sweet on the lips as the beautiful kiss of a boy.

ii.

He found the long-necked ewer in the outer trench.
– It fell to her to cleave into the tomb,

Sudden with the mattock. All at once
Her grassy furrow fell open like a mouth.

Inside somehow the light through ravelling motes
Touched on a long grey tongue so wrapped in silence

At first surprise could not make it exclaim.
Grey, and the golden motes; and then the gold,

Gold of its crown sung out, and its gold slippers,
And were its fingers ringed with gold and firelight?

And were not both its paps great golden targes?
And were its eyes not open, blue and glowing?

Was it not smiling now, with love, with love?
– He found the long-necked ewer in the outer trench.

iii.

To have been dead then, and to have her find him!
To have been lying in the narrow dark
When she first knocked, her arms raised up the mattock
And brought it down right here, beside his heart!

To have been dead when those white arms, whose light
Startled the painless dark awake, those lips
Parted in wonder at such bright things, not persons,
To have been lightly dead, as in a doze

And to come to to her astounding presence,
First silent and then kneeling by his side,
And touching, touching the gold disc that hid his heart
And lifting the blue jewels off his eyes!

And lifted, and the holes were his, and hollow,
And dirt fell through the sockets, the bone shuddered
And the jaw at last fell open; on its stem
The skull averted, hurt, against the light.

iv.

She knelt a minute there before she called the others.
She gazed at bones and gold, it was not him.
Above the grave's brim with its grassy lip

She saw the young man, the ewer in his hands,
How he was bending like a Roman, shirtless,
Luminous, and wavering in the heat.

Her heart was running in her wrists, her temples.
She clutched the two blue gemstones in her fists.
The gold was there, was hers too, to be claimed,
The vertebrae and ribs, sternum and femurs,
The wristbones and the anklebones were hers,
The skull, too, blind, with its broken brow and cheek,

They were hers to map, to brush and photograph,
To lift. Her skeleton, her jewels and heart,
While the outer trench was filling like a cup
With wine, or like a chalice full of blood.
The bones were all hers. So she called out to him
Over the grassy lip, and he came to her.

Amphion

14 February 2005

We live in a paper house.
Your dwelling's made of stone
And mine, a place of brick.
But we live in a paper house.

The walls of our paper house
Are pages ripped from books;
The ceiling's gothic, dark.
We live in a paper house.

The window panes are each
A verse of a poem or lament:
Tears of love gone, or refrained
We live in a paper house

Utterance of grief or loss
From before, when we were apart,
Averting our present heart.
We live in a paper house.

In the New Town it rained.
We dined. Your hand touched mine
Almost. I found my heart.
We live in a paper house.

In Rye we woke to bells
And walked on cobbled streets.
My heart was in my mouth.
We live in a paper house.

At Penshurst, avenues
Of autumn led down to spring,

What was the spell? Your eyes.
We live in a paper house.

Chatsworth, Manchester,
My pulse beat in your wrists
Tense as a verb to keep
Alive in a paper house.

What do we do to turn
The pages of this space
To mortar, brick and stone?
We live in a paper house.

On this page I write home
Made solid, out of stone,
And in it, my dear, the two
Who live in a paper house

Unpack their lives and strike
A fire in the hearth and turn
Their soles to the glow. If now
We live in a paper house,

We can reshape it to
A lantern whose warm glow
Spills on the lawn and the snow.
We live. In a paper house,

Believe me, these hard stones
Light on the tongue like words
Are true, and not for long
We'll live in a paper house

But in a house we build
Of touch, and hours, and napes,

My lips climbing your breast.
The walls of our paper house

At dawn will have turned to a hard
And holding place to be
In love, and heart to heart.
We live in a paper house

Out of whose pages we'll draw
An ample residence.
Folded away we'll keep
The walls and the paper slates

Of the house where once we dwelt
And love transformed to this,
Solid, fabulous.
We lived in a paper house.

Wanting to Think

Why, when I want to think of you, do I think of him?
He may be dead, and yet he still lies with you
Warming his calloused hands between your thighs.
He may still be alive, and his lips for ever
Puckered at your nipple, above your heart.

I want to think about you in my arms, the way we were
For a while. Then he came out of nowhere to stay.
He was tall, and golden, stripped to the waist, when we sawed
And chopped all autumn the firewood, heaped it
Outside your kitchen door. You were always watching;

You patted him on the back and sniffed the air
Pungent with our sweat, you caught his smell.
That autumn, when I lay with you, you started pretending
These hands of mine were his hands in the dark, these lips
His and the tufts in my armpits his and you inhaled

Hungry, pressed against me, pressed against
A man you were imagining in my place:
Shaping, stretching me to fit your bed; no wonder
When I think of you, as I do, each day and night, I think
Of what you were thinking of, how you watched as I watched you,

How as autumn ended, just before you left
That night, noiseless, away with him for good,
I came upon him at twilight in a clearing.
After the weeks we'd mutely worked together,
Till dark we rested in the deep cool grass without a word.

While all the time I loved you, as I love you,
He lay with me and he was satisfied,
I lay with him and not for a minute thought
Of how you watched through the screen door, but only
How musky, how good he smelled, and his hand on my chest.

John Gilpin Eludes the Hunt

Perhaps the saddle slipped,
Not cinched quite tight enough,
Or did he choose to slide
Under the horse as it ran
Away from the hunt and the fox
Whose swift red flare of a brush
Between the combs of wheat
Into the smoky wood
Drew off the lilting dogs,
Red coats and silly hats,
The gentry of the shire?

Whatever was the case
The roan horse rode him rough.
The man hugged its long neck
With both arms and his thighs
Clasped the belly tight.
The horse came out on top
And seemed to ride the man
Faster and further off.
Clattering stone and shale
It fled the hunt as if
The shire was on its tail
And it the vixen whose cub
Clung to her quaking heart.

Up the steep chalk cliff
It pummeled, above the sea
Looking not right or left
It sped, and the breakers broke
In time with its rasping breath.
Over the parching moor
It scattered fiery prints,

Onto a road that swerved
Along a river bank,
Always its head straight out,
And straight out its tail behind
And hung from the missile the man
Clenched tight with desire
Into the final stretch
Where the river borders a rise
Into a pasture field
And sheep and cattle wade
In buttercups and grass.

There with a whinny the horse
Halts. It trembles its mane.
Released from the thundering speed
Reluctantly the man
(John Gilpin is his name)
First with his tingling knees
Then untwining his arms
Gently lets go the horse.
He drops and rolls like a stone
Into the summer grass.
The horse lies down beside
And places its frothing head
Giant and full of love
Against the rider's curve,
Against his cheek and his heart.
They lie in the sun and breathe.
Around them sheep and cattle
Nuzzle the sweet blades.

Far off somewhere a horn
Bleats, and the blood red fox
Is torn like an old coat
By hounds, and the hunt goes home.

Victor Casasola, Photographer

He was present when they brought in the thirteen boys,
Don Victor Casasola, photographer for
La Semana Ilustrada: 'Truth in Photographs';
Present in his smudged sepia suit, his camera
Stout and square on three oak legs, quite sturdy,
And the lad who bore the flash and the tube and chain
Was present also, though it was past midnight.
They had been busy: a dozen square glass plates
In the box already: mug shots of some drunks,
One with a fresh machete slash on his cheek;
A clutch of prostitutes they'd gathered in
All for his camera, they swore and shouted; a burglar
(If he was a burglar) sullen and grey and thin,
The kind who might pour himself through a keyhole
Or under a crack in the door.

                              In this shot,
Ranged along a stained wall two, three deep,
The boys are laughing, or they try to laugh:
Don Victor has vanished under his long black cloth.
He bobs up and down like a bride of death in her veil,
And through the finder
He sees them upside-down and black and white.
Still! he commands
And for ever on the glass plate they are:
The pretty one (Gabriel) thrusts his hip forward
And grins to sell his wit, his lovely eyes;
Raul is pouting; five turn away or hide,
Invisible but you infer their laughter; the eighth
Stands tall and burly as an acrobat, his biceps ripe,
His singlet shows his hard pecs round as targets.
He wears a man's moustache and is almost a man.
And him – the unfortunate, who was hurrying home
Late from work, his mother waiting supper for him,

Corralled by the officers, hauled in with the rest.
Dropped out of his life into this picture,
He stares from the edge bemused. Opposite
Necessity and Hunger (Castor and Pollux, bright stars)
Are here because they had nowhere to go.
They smirk, maybe they smell food or money.

In this shot how sweet and absurd the young men are,
All herded here, maricas, locas, mariposas,
So lovely, alive, so young: since 1935
Not a day has passed. For good they hang suspended
Between desire and terror. The plate preserves
Every nuance of their nightliness:
The smell of sweat and hair grease and perfume,
Of cigarette smoke perched in a roach on the lip,
Preserves the juke box rattling the bar opposite
And through the open door to the portales
The chill blows in.
                    Don Victor
Finishes, is satisfied, packs the camera up,
Sets the homburg low on his brow, the lad
Gathers the flash stuff, tube and chain, they smile,
Joke with the chief, the officers, shake hands,
A fist of money and an open palm,
Ignore the boys, pull the door to as they go.
The air grows still. The room grows dark with silence.

After a minute, *Follow them, go*, says the chief
And the acrobat cannot believe his luck.
He pushes forward and struts smiling, surprise, relief,
Almost reaches the door. The shot goes in
Low at the back and a different kind of surprise
Brightens his face, he clutches his belly, out
Through his fingers surges brilliant urgent blood
Playful, in chugs that are heartbeat, heartbeat, heartbeat.

The next shot, a bullet into a heart,
And after, to a head, two to a groin,
To a throat, a liver, to an eye, to an ear.
That pretty one (Gabriel) they spare, they drag him
Down to the cells, the other inmates have him.

The one boy left they make hideous with a knife,
Slice his nose and genitals and shove him
Out of the nightmare into the night; and cool
Almost-dawn is in the streets. On all fours walking
A mile and a half on his blood, as if a stream, a smear,
He makes his way back to the corner of Calle Humboldt
And Articulo 123, where the water truck

Is spraying the cobbles and the sweepers are at work
And the streetlamps dim, the sky turns bruise from black.
Five hours ago the boys were larking, dancing
For fun or money or the two together.
They laughed and teased the passers-by. A camera
Lay in wait; a camera took them. Took them in.
The boy lies down at the kerb, tucks his knees up,
That one boy only who stepped clear of the frame.
The sweepers sweep around him and day breaks.

Erebus and Terror

Hamnavoe, 1845

It was damp and chill that autumn, the stone scum-mossy.
Two ships moored at the cobbled quay, their last
Old world landfall, to take provisions.
They stayed a fortnight and the sun came out,
Scapa shone like a silver sheet, so they stayed on
A day longer, another, and if the men
Had had their way they'd be there still in rotting hulls,
Merry, with long white beards, hobbling, alive.
They were not minded – the crew, the meagre men –
To sail beyond and over the rim of the world.

Sir John Franklin was Ulysses and Ahab in one,
Hired by the Hudson Bay to finish tracing
The North West Passage to the other ocean.
Gagged in Eton collar, he was correct,
High-pitched, severe, with tourniquets at the wrists,
All black and white, steel toe and spangle boots.

The crew saw, gazing south to the swelling Cullags of Hoy
Or east to Fara, Burray, Lambholm, or north along
The solid isle of Hrossey that this was the very end
Of *terra firma*, where it crumbles into islands
And the young men and cabin boys desired
A season here, or a year in lengthening daylight
With bright-eyed women watching them as they swung
Shirtless and wild-hearted in the rigging, or bashful
Came ashore for grog. The women asked them
In lilty Norse accents why *Erebus*, why *Terror*.
What could they answer? It was the owners' whim
Who stayed in London, conversed among themselves
And swaggered to their Clubs to read the Lists.

The tall ship was the Roman underworld; *Terror*,
Squat, graceless, Jehovah's wrath and will.

The young men could have stayed in the bright falling weather
And nights with the Aurora Borealis
Stammering echo, echo light to the Pole, from the Pole,
And they would have done so but for their starched Ahab,
But for the pull of money and the tide,
Both cold and out of sight colluding with him,
Current, currency, not to be dammed, diverted,
And a whole huge empire pink from end to end
Afloat on coin and ocean, blood and lymph
Of sailors, soldiers, native folk who lived and died
Wherever the currents took the ships, the guns,
Calicos and bayonets, beads, buttons,
Trinkets and smallpox, to pick off islands,
Mainlands, devour frailer kingdoms, empires.

One Friday the cannon sounded, the ships at last
Upped anchor, hoisted canvas, eased out between
The lips of Hoy Sound, Warbeth Bay and Graemsay;
The islands dwindled and set, the two ships caught
And held a following wind for Canada.
So they went, and four months after both went under
The ice with all hands, every one, at the helm
Sir John who in his pockets bore a fortune
In notes promissory, a map with blanks
And cross-hatched where no Christian had set foot or sail:
He was to sketch in land and channels; in his waistcoat
A purse fat with cold-hearted sovereigns.

They went under. But was it with all hands?
What did the men do when the last cold suns
Were setting on the ice, and huge slabs slid
Out of the towering glaciers into the sea and buoyed them
A little along, a little further along from home,

From the hope of home, what did they do? They were so
Hungry then, so ravenous and their knives
Sharp because they had been honing them,
There was nothing else to do. What did they do?

The men did not draw lots, but *Erebus* and *Terror*
Limped side by side through the floes, with glimmering cook fires,
The captain kept to his quarters, silently
The crews consumed the cabin boys, the boatswains –
One by one – the ones too weak or junior,
Who on the wide Atlantic crossing sang as they swabbed the deck
Or like birds chirped in the rigging, hand over hand,
And hailed to and fro, the youngsters, the young brothers
Out for the thrill of it, to learn the elements and be
Not like men but men indeed.
                                   Then the fires were out
And all that was tender and good washed down with snow,
The bones overboard, there was nothing left to do
And the hulls froze fast and did not sink until spring.

The Inuit sold the captain's powder horn
To John Rae, the Orkney fur trader, years later, ivory
From another imperial climate; they sold the octant,
The waistcoat, braces and belt, a pewter snuff box
With a Georgian hunting scene, and a silver
Locket with three blonde curls of a child or lover.

The Golden Dome

22 February 2006

I was there once, oh, forty years ago.
The map does it no justice: the river's sluggish,
Forgetful; the ruins of the great
City of Samarra are drab and crusted, but what you see
From miles off approaching is the dome, the golden
Dome, rising above the Tigris like a moon…

Among the elaborate geometries that praised
The Merciful, the Compassionate (in His name),
Not far from the spiral minaret that screws the earth
Right into heaven so the muezzin's voice,
Even as men can hear it, talks to God,
Al-Mutawakkil set a rectangle (measured it out,
Being a tall man, pacing as a king,
His servants and architects drawn in his wake)
Two hundred forty deep, a hundred sixty
Wide. His slaves began to build
Fortress-thick walls with bricks of clay
Washed by the Tigris, hardened in the sun,
Ribbed the structure with forty four stalwart towers
Until it rose higher than the highest house,
Even than the highest house of God.

Within, the blue and gold arcade was exquisite,
With tracery and the words the Prophet said
Woven, inwoven like a choir of birds.
Eloquent especially were the arches facing Mecca.
Compassion, Mercy had an open gate there.
Malwiya was the mosque's own minaret:
If Al-Mutawakkil paced his way to heaven
Malwiya was the first phase of his journey,

Fifty-two paces up into the sky. When it was done
It was the great mosque of Islam. Samarra.
'Not briefly the Abassids were approved by heaven.'

It grew, it was remembered and forgotten.
Nasr al-Din Shah, so God would see him,
And re-bless Samarra with His ancient favour,
Gave the gold dome, though not in Nasr's lifetime
Did its hemisphere crescent the horizon.
A century ago, under Muzaffar al-Din Shah
It was done: gold on the outside, inside
It was just like a blue night sky, a replica
Of heaven itself. Man honoured God by making
A second home for him.
                                          At each corner, the square,
Bearing the tonnes of dome – clay, tile and gold –
Hosted ornate and very holy graves,
Of Imam Ali al-Naqi (the tenth, peace to him),
His son Hasan al-Askari (the eleventh, peace),
Hakimah Khatoon, Ali's dearest sister,
And finally the grave of fair Nargis Khatoon,
Mother of Imam al-Mahdi (peace on them all).

Those were the great men, caliph, builder, imams,
The great men and their shadows, mother, sister.
Of the brick makers and slaves there is no record
Except the thing they did, which was well done.

It is the hour of morning prayer.
The square is full of white doves, pouting, preening,
And men with low-arched feet, the poor believers,
The ones who carry God on their bent shoulders
And kneel and touch their foreheads to the ground
And empty out their purses when they go,
All dressed in white too like the plump amorous doves.

As they are praying, murmuring, standing, bowing,
Their eyes fixed towards Mecca and the truth,
They do not sense concealed behind the ornate tombs
Four brothers equal in their other faith.
They do not see the signal, suddenly
The dead Imams (peace to them) and their shadows
Burst from their stone in splinters, heaven falls
In great gouts of lapis, clay and gold
And as when Samson regrew his hair
And rattled the columns, down the temple fell.

Among the sirens and the modern sounds
The shadows come, shadows in their black gowns,
Veiled, but their veils awry and wet with weeping,
The shadows gather and their eyes are red,
Their wailing louder than the circling copters.
Out of those shadows came the caliphs once,
And come the little warriors, the brick-makers and builders,
Out of the shadows come calligraphers
Who write the names of God in tile and gold,
Out of them come the mystics and the Imams,
And lovers, and more shadows like themselves, too,
Some beautiful like Hakimah and Nargis.

The martyrs gloat together as they rise
Past Malwiya and gazing down observe
The gibbous wreck, the great dome broke,
Dust in a plume and a cloud and a haze then settling.
Around the wreck a swarm; as they go higher
Samarra is an anthill, though they hear
Even as they pass into Paradise
The wailing shadows, so like the ones they left
Wherever it is they came from and are gone;
And since their men are dead, the shadows
Here and there, wherever, having spent
Their generations in giving, take flesh, become.

Regression

1 August 2006

Riddled he was, and idling, Sebastian,
Bound to the trunk by laughter and desire.
The missiles struck, their feathered ends
Glittering, the beaks like acupuncture pins
Releasing wheels of lightness, lightness, light.

Such was his faith, grace gave him cheerfulness:
In each bright eye love planted an arrow stem,
And in the throat, too, a shaft that like a bird
Bubbled and shrilled, the air and phlegm escaping;
Bound hand and foot, his mouth crammed full of rag,

It was his means of singing hymn and psalm
As all the pagan weapons flooded down
The blue air towards him, Christ's first porcupine.

      * * *

Make light of him? I do make light of him.
I watched my comrades one by one take aim;
I did not draw my bow, I watched him shimmer;
And saw them gag him, saw them bind him to
That stripped trunk with wire taken from the trench;

I saw them find him on his knees in prayer
Asking his God about the coming battle;
I watched him kneel, I watched him cross himself,
I watched him kiss his mother; the soldiers seized him;
The soldiers marched up hill and gathered men

That last evening of harvest when the streets
Were full before the drums of harvest home

And he was not the only man they snared there.

I watched him grow from boyhood on the hills
High above where St George slew the dragon;
This is how once upon a time it was.
The ocean washes a broad shore, olive groves
Climb ancient terraces, lemons, oranges

And where the cyclamen with their small purples
Emit a Tyrian scent like sweetest sounds,
And in harsh friendly habitations clinging
As hamlets named for saints, sultans and kings,
Babies are cradled, there are marriages.

Make light of him, who came from such a summit,
Washed his little feet as a boy in the broad
Bay that opened out its fan towards Europe,

      * * *

Make light of one who loved the minarets
And temple courts, church towers of Fez, Shemlan,
And loved the festivals, and he could dance,
Who had a sweetheart when they came for him.
He loved his comrades, too, in time. In time

He learned to love his foes and had to die.
I watched them bend him round the broken tree
Early in the day, before the sun,
Before opponents primed the dawn's barrage,
Before the world tuned in with blank, cold eye.

I watched him die, my comrades one by one
Wiping their eyes (they loved him), drawing taut
Their bow strings, letting fly. Then back to battle.

I stayed behind, unwired him, eased him down.
I stretched him in a grave and wondered what
To say above the wreckage of such grace,
As if a landscape had been turned to salt,
Or a high temple felled by a blind old fool,

As if Christ had once more been pinned to a beam,
As if the Jews of Europe again on a pyre
Burned like the cattle, sheep and pigs of Britain.
As if the poor Jews of the ghetto trembled,
As if the smoke from those straight chimneys bore

Like muezzins' voices or the peel of bells
Something to heaven that belonged to it.
I pulled the quills in fistfuls from my chest.

Notes for the Cactus Poem

The teddy bear cholla and the fat fat

*

Oh buckthorn, devil, whipple, teddy bear

*

Oh beavertail, oh pancake, porcupine

*

Oh plump saguaro with your hairy arms, I love
Each of you with a different nerve of heart.
Especially you, so trim, so pert, your birds
Cupped in your pits and crotches, little friends

*

Oh areoles and aureoles, the orioles
With yellow caps are havering and hot
Making themselves a breeze with their cut wings

*

I ask the docent and he indicates

*

Oh nation, how you might have been, spread from
So sure an order, with such tendering love

Inordinate Desires

*'I believe it would go ill with many of us, if we were faced with a
strong temptation, and I suspect that with many of us it does go ill.'*
Ivy Compton Burnett

He set out on the innocent exodus. He went at Easter
In a lengthening dawn, and he did not count the days.
He was young. With the wooden comb his mother made him
He parted his hair in the middle (his beard was slow).
He was fair still, he glowed like a source of light.

There were so many priests about, there was too much singing;
He did not like God the Father who came from Rome
With his tattered son and the incomprehensible bird.
Easter for him was other kinds of rebirth,
But from the trees and streams, the uplands and valleys
He knew the native spirits dislodged, crowding the shore
To cross over like no longer immortal souls, lined up
Awaiting the ferry and the disgruntled boatman.
They did not intend to fade out to the sound of bells and choiring;
They would find a new woodland or water for haunt, untroubled
By candles and books and the tedious, meaningless Latin.

Without farewell before daybreak he left home.
He pushed past the almost visible crowd on the shore,
Divine shapes, scents, their sorrowful voices and silence.
He murmured out of respect and they let him pass through.
Goodbye he declared to them and to his country.

First he crossed the small sea in a leather coracle
Pointing the blunt prow at what looked like mainland.
The sea was glassy, he paddled with his palms, at landfall
Made fire and warmed them, conjuring spirits of a new place.
They gathered around to gaze at his lovely body.
He abandoned his boat and clambered up the rocks.

He climbed a hill, a ridge, and then a mountain.
It was a protracted joy, that crossing away
From the small sea. Looking back, Ireland got littler,
Then it and the smooth water were lost to view
And never again did he see what had been home,
Hear its lilt, or receive news of his many brothers
Who bred, and banked their fields, who fished and hunted,
And made a tribe, a village and a nation.

The uplands were lush and full of fauna, the grass
Deep, humming, and everywhere were gods,
Their tears, their wounds and resurrections. Spring
Smattered the glades, flecked and mottled with blossom,
The wheeling birds shouted their emphatic prayer;
And deer: that enormous stag with a broken antler;
Wolves and wild cats, too, a bear he saw, red pheasants,
And rooting through an oak wood, a tusky boar…

He walked in amazement (he did not count the days)
Reading the symbols, and cheerful local gods
Skipped and tumbled before him, showing the way
Across the very backbone of that mainland.
It was not England yet. It was wilderness.
He wrapped his feet in grass and leaves, in strips of leather;
He wore a leathern kilt and a stiff hide waistcoat
Fragrant with wear and weather. As he went along
He runed, was merry, it was almost like rhyming.
He climbed jet black mountains veined with silver falls,
Washed face and hands in the frenzied spray of those tarns,
Made the noises of a man free now of Christendom,
In the uncharted, unmarred wilderness, his sweet voice
Gracing the ears of insects, beasts and wild fowl
And the ears of the local spirits, Orpheus,
Or as Adam's must have done when he told the animals
Who they were in the first sunrise of the world,
Before Eve had been carved out of his rejoicing

To correct and contradict him, and the tall fruit tree
Stood safe in his obedience, when at evening
God himself, not his bloodied Son, walked out in starlight
And kissed his creature, and lay with him in the dark.

It was not, he began to know, an innocent exodus.
It was the long route to exile, the way that hermits
Took to white martyrdom, alone with their God for ever.
He was not like them: wild-hearted spirits of place
Coaxed his credulous footsteps past the equinox.

On the eastern shore of what was becoming England
He saw far off kernels of cities, squat towers, spires;
Rough roads north and south, wagons groaning with stone,
And into meagre harbours boats and barges
Hugging the coast bore produce in and away.
That world was not for him, with its crosses and crossroads.

He saw steep islands dark in a bigger sea,
No man mark on them, no smoke, no stone quarry,
No furrows or shepherds, in their thin woods no traps.
It was summer now (he did not count the days),
He sat on the summit of the last hill and looked east
Wondering where on that island he would build
His round stone dwelling and give his mortal days
To local grace, the gods of leaf and stone,
With his soul configured to love, like a hearth, his heart
On fire but unconsumed because such promiscuous heat
Amazes and makes not cinders but rapture and language.
His dwelling would be a beacon, a land-star radiant
To a lowering ocean unbroken beyond the islands
As far as the eye. Shading his eyes, he went on his way.

He crossed the bad sands not knowing they were bad
Between two tides, two islands, walking ankle deep, knee,
Then up to the waist, the paps, until only his upturned face

65

Floated on the water, the mouth crying out joyful spells,
Eyes fixed on the sun, the flaxen hair fanned out
Like rays of a lesser sphere. He could not swim
But there was no need, a sea god hovered ahead,
Sandals firm on the wave.
                                        Emerging step by step
He was new, it was autumn, his homelessness
This island, these tilting rocks. He chose for his dwelling
A high place with a view of nothing but east,
The rows of waves impatient to crash on the boulders,
Where the storms might climb and burst over his reflections,
And the fowls of the air become familiars.

He set to work carting stones, gods gathered nearby
Harkening, making crowns of nettle, spears of bone,
A cup from a gourd, and a dish. Each day his dwelling
Grew higher, like a hive for bees, a dome, a cranium.
One day, it was the solstice, a final stone
Closed the fontanel. The votary moved in.
He gathered the crowns and spears, the cup and dish
And laid out the new table for his guests.

Would the gods sit down beside at his first supper?
He looked for them, he called out praising their names.
They had all gone off somewhere. There was nowhere to go!
The tide was full and even the deep route hither
Had gone under waves, the mainland had vanished in fog.
He sat alone at his table. He sat alone.
The gods who had brought him were gone. He started counting.
Day one was the day when things began to go.

He watched his shadow every morning, lengthening
Over the water, over the sand and stones,
And being washed and parched like a piece of laundry
Until it was white as a nightshirt spread to dry
On a gorse bush, fluttering a little, an empty sleeve,

Saying go on, go back, go on, go back
The way waves do, the way the tides do, also,
Or simply wind blows and the tide says nothing at all.

How clean the stones and the sand, the breaking waves,
How clean the moonlight, the sunlight, and his lovely throat
Young and in love – is it still young and in love? –
With the spirits, his voice pure as a bird's, but he's counting,
The days are shortening, his voice is growing darker.
Surely they listen out and watch their votary
There on the verge of the cliff in his careful dance
Like a gull whose wings are reliance, like a guillemot.

So he chanted, he praised and danced, and it was the end
Of autumn. For the first time cold, he felt the bones in his flesh.
Above him, north, with terror he saw the Lights
And it was a human shadow that towered in them,
A man on a cross, a man with a cross inside him
Instead of a skeleton; the cross was still and shimmered
As if it held its breath so as to observe him.

He was trembling, he saw the ghostly limbs
Behind the bright-dim curtain, those long wired veins
Through which pulse flickered and the wine flowed,
The chest breathed with almost no sound at all.
This figure had nothing to do with the gods who brought him,
Tugged at his heart, took their leave when most he needed.
This looked like the son of the god he had sought to elude,
Now a giant surveying a world and a singular man
Abandoned by everything he'd served, but nonetheless
Dancing and shivering above the scrum of waves.

Cities had grown on the mainland meanwhile, monks and priors
Grew fat; there were nuns and teachers, the farmsteads prospered.
The places he'd passed through had roads now, stone towers and walls,
Where he'd chanted to wilderness out of a pagan heart.

To the east there is nothing. The sleet blows in.
It is so cold now, winter hardening.
The days are counted and are counting down.
After laud and joy, the radiance fading,
Winter is here, and bidding becomes of the body,
The rings of light, of fire, the rings of starlight.
The votary tries his tongue to find what he means,
He tries to speak with what has been refined.
He has no words at all. The feet that led, the hands
That rested on his head, arrested him, are nowhere.
He was grown old and unremarkable, and now
He knows desire. He knows desire as he has never
Known any passion in his person before, he desires
A voice, a touch. From his precipice soon
Like a gannet he's to dive, or like a stone.

Winter has come indeed, and the stars, he's wasted, wasted.
No devil arrives to offer long life and kingdoms,
To touch his brow, to kiss him on the lips.
No gods return with prayer mats and chains of flowers,
With brands and blankets, with warm thick drinks, with lamplight,
With meat or fruit, with a breathing loaf or a lamb.
(In the coldest night someone does cover him
And when he wakes he finds
A fire alive in the hearth, his table laid
With biscuit, and in the gourd a mouthful of pure water.)

He is old, his matted beard dark, filthy. He has
Praised presence and absence and set his glow
Fading on the island's seaward face. When he starts dying,
That night, in the flickering of his chamber,
The Vikings steer five ships packed with warriors
Around the end of his island, using his glimmer
As lighthouse and marker, reaching their intended haven.

Had he survived that night, even afar he'd have felt
The heat of the conflagration, smelled apocalypse
As the pagans returned and the little gods came with them,
Clapping their hands and rejoicing, and rushed to the woods
To be with their trees and streams and hills and valleys
As the church spires collapsed, the monks and priors and priests
Fuel for bonfires, and until the Vikings withdrew
They were safe, divine again, though the shuddering Lights
Disclosed the tall cross and the watcher, smoke in his heart.

The island's dark, the darker now for his dying,
Unmarked and unremarked. But someone covers his face,
Is winding in coarse scented cloth the extinguished body,
Having tidied the wild hair, parted it in the centre,
And washed at last the limbs that longed to be touched.
Someone rolls them to the cliff edge, lets them go east.